99 DOs and DON'Ts with open adoption

99 DOs and DON'Ts with open adoption

RUSSELL ELKINS

99 DOs and DON'Ts with Open Adoption
What Hopeful Adoptive Parents Need to Know Before Adopting a Baby
part 4 of the series: 30 Minute Guides to Headache-Free Open Adoption Parenting
By Russell Elkins
©2019 Russell Elkins

series line editors: Kim Foster, Jenna Lovell
series content editors: Martin Casey, Cathy Watson Childs

Cover photo and author photo by Jammie Elkins Photography
Cover design by Inky's Nest Design
Interior book layout by Inky's Nest Design

ISBN: 978-1-950741-08-3

Inky's Nest Publishing

RussellElkins.com
2nd edition
First edition printed in 2015 in the United States of America

1. Don't disregard your own feelings.

You are in a unique situation. Few people have ever been in your shoes even if they have adopted before. There will likely be many people around you willing to share their thoughts. There is nothing wrong with that, but do not let others overrule your opinion. Only you know all of the details of your situation, and your opinion is what matters. If your mother or your best friend do not agree with you, they will have to come to terms with it.

2. Do ask your child's birthparents how they are feeling.

You cannot assume to know whether they are comfortable in certain situations. They are going through something you cannot fully understand because you have never been in their shoes. This means that they may feel uncomfortable at times you do not expect.

You also cannot assume they are happy with their overall situation. You must ask them from time to time. You may be surprised by something you hear.

3. *Don't try to be the birthparents' only support.*

No matter how much your child's birthparents love you, they need other people around them to lift them up. You may feel like you are responsible for helping their heart heal since you, as an adoptive parent, were on the receiving end of what caused them so much pain. It is a good thing to be there for them. You have the ability to help lift them up and make their life better, but you also must encourage them to share their burden with others from their inner circle—their best friend, mother, other birthparents. You cannot be all of these things for them.

4. *Don't worry if your family does not understand open adoption.*

Open adoption is a new concept that did not become common practice until after the turn of the century. This means that a lot of people still do not fully understand it. Many continue to view adoption through the eyes of yesteryear when adopted children did not have contact with their biological roots. Do your best to educate those close to you, but do not expect everyone to latch onto the concept. If you choose an open adoption, some people will disagree with your decision. It is probably safe to say that someone will strongly disagree with your decision no matter what you decide, so make your own decisions and do not worry what others think.

5. Don't forget how hard Mother's Day was before you adopted.

This also goes for Father's Day, the weekend of your church group's Father-and-Son's campout, Mother-Daughter day at work, etc. There is a good chance someone near you is struggling with infertility. Many of these people are uncomfortable receiving a rose on these special days because they do not want a gift out of pity, they feel uncomfortable around all the happy mothers, or they just wish the day could be over. If you have battled infertility, then you are in a position where your experiences and ability to empathize might actually mean something to them. Take some time to think about those around you who struggle with infertility, and consider reaching out to them. You just might be a light for them on an otherwise dark day.

6. *Don't ever feel entitled to someone else's baby.*

No matter how badly you want to be a parent, and no matter attached you feel to a child, you can never consider that child to be rightfully yours until everything is final through the legal system. Being contacted by an expecting mother, even if she has promised to place her baby with you, does not make that baby yours. The birthparents have every right to change their mind until the legal process is finished.

Not only is it wrong to refer to someone else's baby as yours before the child is part of your family, but it will drive a wedge between you and the biological parents that can be difficult to overcome. This does not mean you should not become attached. You should. It just means that you should not let yourself get to a point where you feel someone owes you a child.

7. *Don't throw a social media party in front of the birthparents.*

If you are not connected with the birthparents on social media, by all means you should rejoice and share the excitement online. But if they have access to your social media page, such as Facebook, be careful not to rub your excitement in their face. Chances are good they will see every word of it. Remember that these same things that bring you so much joy are a result of a separation that is likely causing the birthparents a lot of pain.

8. *Do talk about who will hold the baby.*

Especially when the child is still young, some adoptive parents do not like to give the birthparents time to hold the baby, and other adoptive parents want to insist they do. Every birthparent is different, so you must communicate about these things. Do they want to hold the child a lot? Are they uncomfortable holding the child too much?

It is also important to understand that your feelings are just as important. If the birthparents want to hold the child during the entire visit, but it hurts you to not have a turn, then you need to communicate that with them. If your needs are ignored, you may develop an aversion to your adoption relationship. Everyone is important in the adoption triad.

9. *Don't exaggerate about the birthparents.*

The child you adopted will have a lot of questions over the years about their biological family. Do not make the birthparents sound as if they are saints, and do not talk about them like they are devils. Be real. Birthparents are normal, real people. Help your child learn to love their biological roots, but you will not be doing your child any favors by warping their understanding of the truth. They will form their own relationship and opinion someday.

10. *Don't compare your adoption to others'.*

Your adoption is unique. There are no other situations out there with your combination of birthparents, adoptive parents, and the child. It does not matter if someone else's adoption is more open or closed than yours. It does not matter how often someone else has visits or sends pictures. You only need to concern yourself about the adoption in front of you. And if you are fortunate to adopt more than once, you cannot expect your other adoptions to be like your first. A different set of birthparents as well as a different child will change the dynamics of your adoption situation.

12

11. Don't expect all birthparents to want to send an equal number of gifts.

It is nearly impossible to establish consistency with gift-giving. The birthfather may want to shower his biological daughter with gifts while the birthmother does not want to send anything, or the other way around. Sometimes it is the birth grandma who wants to send a bunch.

If you have adopted more than once, there is a good chance one biological family will send more gifts than another. How will your children feel if one of them gets a ton of awesome gifts from birthfamily members and the other child gets nothing? Some people ask the birthfamilies not to send any gifts because of this reason, but gifts can be a great way to show love. My wife and I have asked our children's birthfamilies to consider both of our children if they want to send gifts and that has worked well for us.

12. Don't expect a long visit with birthparents to be like a long visit from your other family members.

Face-to-face visits can be a special experience. Some adoptions are so open that a birthparent who has to travel a long distance to visit will stay in the adoptive family's home.

13

If you plan to do this, keep in mind that the relationship you have with your child's birthparents is not the same as you may have with, say, your aunt or grandma. You many consider all of these people to be part of your family, but there is an innate level of intensity that comes with an open adoption relationship. You clean your house when your mother-in-law comes to stay, but you scrub your house twice when the birthmother comes. Adoptive parents tend to want to prove to the birthparents that choosing them to parent the child was the right choice. That naturally carries along with it a need to perform at your best. You cannot keep that up forever. It will exhaust you even if the visit goes well.

This need to prove yourself will ebb over time, but these visits can still have an elevated level of intensity. Your child will pick up on this intensity. When a child is exposed to an intense situation for an extended period of time, even if those intense feelings are positive, they have a tendency to become exhausted. And when children are exhausted they act out. Their emotional stability is thrown off.

This will put you in a difficult situation. Your child is used to being corrected or disciplined a certain way, but how will you handle a temper tantrum if it happens right in front of a birthparent? Would you handle things the way you always do, or will you be worried they may think you are being too harsh? Even if you handle it perfectly, how comfortable would the birthparents be to see their biological child kicking and screaming on the floor like every three-year-old will do on occasion?

Face-to-face visits can be some of the most rewarding times you can spend together. There is nothing more intimate. If these types of visits are part of your open adoption, come up with a plan for how long a visit should last. Make it appropriate to your child, taking into consideration your child's age and maturity. Do not push these visits too long or things could get intense and uncomfortable for the latter part of the visit. These visits can be a beautiful thing, but it is possible to have too much of a beautiful thing.

13. Do read other people's adoption stories.

Along with this series of adoption books, I am also the author of the *Glass Half-Full Adoption Memoirs* series. The three books in that series are dedicated to telling our story. I did not write any of these books thinking they could ever make me rich (they will not). I wrote them out of my love for adoption. I always tell people that the best way to prepare for an adoption is to read other people's stories. Experiences are always the best teacher and the closest thing to actually living through an adoption is to have someone tell you their entire story. Upon reading it, you will be able to ask yourself how you would feel and how you would react if you were in our shoes. I cannot count the number of times someone has told me, "I had no idea..." after reading our story.

14. *Don't post anything on social media you would not want the birthparents to read.*

Even if your child's birthparents are not connected to your social media page, it is a good rule of thumb to never post anything about the birthparents you would not say to their face. These types of things have a tendency to weave their way through the social media world and find their way to the very people you are talking about. If you are ever in doubt, even if your comment is not mean, just do not type it. Too many people today think they have to post all of their thoughts for the world to read. You don't. When your mind is stuck on something sensitive, do not use social media as your outlet. Call you sister on the phone. Walk next door and talk to your neighbor. Just do not air out your mental laundry on the internet and expect it to stay contained.

This is especially true with public forums. There are a lot of public forums on Facebook and other sites where people can come together to discuss adoption. People share stories on these pages, voice frustrations, and offer advice. My wife and I used to run one of these pages and we had a number of people post something thinking others from their adoption triad would not see it, and we have seen things turn out badly because of it.

15. *Do learn to share, but also learn to keep some things sacred.*

You are part of an open adoption, which means you are sharing some of the most intimate parts of your life with someone you probably did not know a few years ago. But you do not have to share every little thing. Not only is it okay to keep some experiences for yourself, but it is healthy to do so. You do not have to invite the birthparents to your child's baptism if you do not want to. They do not have to be present at your child's first birthday party if you want that all for yourself. It is okay. You are not a selfish person if you want some things just for you. Be open and *communicate* about these things. It is a good thing to feel "normal" now and then, and "normal" people do not have to invite people to things if they do not want to.

16. *Don't ever lie to the biological father to keep him away.*

Unfortunately, it is not uncommon for the biological father to be kept on the sidelines or out of the picture completely. Sometimes his reputation is tainted by the biological mother's view of him, especially since adoptive families tend to communicate more with her during the process. Treat him with the same respect you would the biological mother. If they do not get along, you may need to have separate relationships with them, never talking to one about the other. An active birthfather can be a wonderful and healthy part of an open adoption. Many of them just need a chance or an invitation.

17. Do understand that your inner circle is easier to control.

If you have a lot of people intimately involved in your open adoption you will have less control of over your situation. You may spend a good amount of effort educating and involving your closest confidantes about your life, but you only see Crazy Uncle Joe once a month. You cannot control the things he says, and he may say something terrible to the birthparents when you are not listening. There are so many delicate moving parts to every open adoption that sometimes it is best to keep things as simple as you can with fewer of your friends involved.

18. *Don't judge your child's birthparents.*

Their personal life is just that—theirs. Do not act like you are their parents. Do not look down your nose at them if they make bad decisions. If the decisions they make ever become dangerous or damaging to your child, then you will have to make some tough decisions about how open your relationship should be, but love them for who they are.

19. *Don't pressure your kids into cuddling.*

Some kids love to snuggle. Other kids do not. Sometimes it is as simple as that. Do not force them to cuddle up to their birthmother just so you can feel good about your situation. Your intentions may be good by thinking you are encouraging your child to bond, but forcing them to sit on a birthparent's lap may have the opposite effect than what you are hoping for. Your child's discomfort could develop an aversion to the birthparents if they feel forced into things.

20. Do consider the birthparents to be family, not competition.

The birthparents play a role in your child's life that you will never be. That is okay. The fact that you are not the only one who exists in their heart does not mean you are less important. They are not your competition. They are family. You have the same goals.

21. Do understand that the relationship will change.

The relationship you built with the biological parents before the birth will inevitably be different from what you will have afterward. Your relationship six months after placement will be different than it was in the beginning. Your relationship will be different six years down the road than it was six months after placement. These changes are normal and should be expected. These changes also mean you have a need to communicate so everyone's changing needs can be addressed.

Expect things to change when your child becomes more independent. The biological parents will probably get married someday and have their own kids. You may begin a new job or move to a new city. Life happens. People progress. These are all good things. Be open to change.

22. Don't be offended if the birthparents friends do not acknowledge you.

If you follow each other's Facebook pages, or if you ever find yourself among the birthparents' friends and family, understand that many of them will not think of you as the child's parents. This is especially evident on social media where you will see comments from people you do not know. Even though they are aware you have adopted this child, they may not feel any connection to you at all. They see the baby their friend gave birth to, and they may talk like you do not exist.

23. Don't agree to an open adoption if you do not want to.

Believe it or not, some birthparents prefer to have little to no contact with the adoptive family. It is okay to say you do not want an open relationship, but it is not okay to agree to an open adoption if you are not truly interested in keeping your promises. Be honest. Take this relationship seriously.

24. Don't expect to just "get over" your jealousies.

Birthparents and adoptive parents all have reason to be jealous of one another. Both sides are something the other is not. You must embrace the things you are rather than focus on what you are not. Otherwise, you will run the risk of resenting the birthparents for being something you cannot be. You are an adoptive parent. You are special.

25. Do celebrate your friends' pregnancies.

Be careful not to let your insecurities and frustrations with infertility take over your life. It may hurt to see your best friend get pregnant for the fifth time, especially if her recent pregnancy was not planned, but do not let that affect you. You are being called to something different now, and your calling in life is not inferior to theirs. You may be sad that you will not experience certain things, but you will have other awesome experiences they will never have. If you learn to celebrate others' pregnancies with them, you will have an easier time coming to terms with your infertility. That is easier said than done, I know.

26. *Don't argue nature vs. nurture.*

Too many adoptive parents find it important to argue over which is more important—the genetic makeup of their child or the upbringing. To engage in this debate is to admit your insecurities as a parent. Both nature and nurture are important. Your children are who they are because of the tools they were born with as well as how they learn to use them throughout life. If you learn to embrace the fact that you are an adoptive parent, rather than simply accepting it, you will find a lot of joy in what makes your child unique. I love seeing my son do things that remind me of his birthmother because I love his birthmother. That does not make me any less of a father.

27. *Do keep all correspondence with the biological father if he is not in the picture.*

If the birthfather is nowhere to be found during the adoption process, you should try to find him. Do not take the expecting mother's word for it that he does not want anything to do with the situation. Imagine the nightmare of bringing a child into your home and becoming attached only to find out later that the biological father never gave his consent and now he wants to raise the child. If someone has conveyed to you that he wants nothing to do with the situation, make sure you have a paper trail to prove it. Even if he refuses to respond, a certified letter expressing your intent will be proof that he was given an opportunity. Keeping a paper trail will ensure the biological father is not being lied to and cheated out of his God-given right to parenthood, and it will ensure you have all your legal bases covered if problems arise in the future.

28. Do share pictures in ways that the photos can be printed.

Sharing pictures is one of the most basic forms of open adoption, yet too many people do not understand the need for quality. Do not just send pictures, but send pictures that can be printed. Even if you take your picture with a professional camera, posting it on Facebook will drastically shrink the quality of every picture. Instagram does the same. Taking a picture with your cell phone is a good way to capture something candid on the fly, but not all cell phones take great pictures. Even if your phone does, your phone will shrink the quality before sending it somewhere, so the picture received will not be the same quality as the picture you took. You can send full resolution pictures through email. Creating a blog for pictures will give them a place to see high quality photos and let them choose whether or not to print them. And, of course, do not forget the option of using traditional snail-mail post. You do not have to do this for all pictures, but give them something worthy of print so they can have one for their nightstand or desk at work.

29. Don't do anything that just feels wrong.

You were born with a conscience for a reason. Use it. If a situation ever arises that does not feel right, follow your heart. You do not want to live the rest of your life regretting a decision or feeling like your family was built on something shady.

30. Don't promise the world.

Do not promise anyone the world because you will never be able to deliver it. You have been given the greatest gift one human can give another—parenthood. That gift came to you because someone was willing to sacrifice a part of them to make it happen. This may make you feel like you are so deeply in their debt that you must do everything in your power to pay them back. It may hurt to hear this, but you will never be able to pay them back. When I said that they gave you the greatest gift one human can give another, that also means that you cannot match it. That does not mean that you do not need to give back. You should. But if you promise the world, you are only going to exhaust yourself trying to fulfill that promise. Once you become exhausted, feeling perpetually in debt like you have reached the end of your rope, what decisions will you then make? Make your adoption relationship a priority in your life, but do not ever promise so much that you will crumble trying to fulfill it.

31. *Don't try to be someone you are not.*

Be you. Do not spend too much time focusing on how awesome other people are. People who blog about their adoptions (myself included) tend to show their best side. Being an active part of adoption advocacy on the internet has given me a lot of connections to others like me. I am not exaggerating when I say that every adoptive parent who blogs and advocates, even those who seem to have perfect adoptions, has gone through more than their share of adoption struggles. It is okay to look up to those you admire, but just know they are human too. You are not weak because you struggle. They are human. They do too.

32. *Don't have a baby shower before the child is placed in your home.*

A lot of people will disagree with me on this one, but wait until after placement before you have a baby shower. I have heard too many stories about people who have had adoptions fall through after they were convinced it was a sure thing. Having a baby shower before that baby is yours is playing with fire.

Also, do not invite the biological mother to your baby shower unless you are absolutely certain she wants to be there. Your friends are excited for *you* to be a mother, and they are there to smother *you* with praise and affection in *your* newfound motherhood. I cannot imagine anything more uncomfortable for a new birthmother to go through shortly after the intense emotions of placing a baby for adoption than to sit through that.

33. *Do recognize Birthmother's Day.*

Some birthmothers do not like Birthmother's Day, saying things like, "A birthmother is also a mother. I do not need a day separate from Mother's Day." But many people see Birthmother's Day as a day to acknowledge how special a birthmother is. Find out how your child's birthmother feels about the day. You love her. Show it on this day. Birthmother's Day is the Saturday before Mother's Day.

Unfortunately, at the time of this publication, there is no Birthfather's Day. Every year I hear people make an attempt to create a day for it, but every year it fails to gain traction. Hopefully that will change someday, but until then you should still find a time around Father's Day to acknowledge your child's birthfather. He is special too.

34. Do come up with a formalized plan for your open adoption.

Some states require hopeful adoptive couples and expecting parents to create a formal plan for their adoption relationship and to put it in writing. Although these plans are not always enforceable by law, I wish all states required them. Failing to have this formal meeting is akin to saying that you will figure things out as you go along. Do not be foolish enough to think you will be on the same page as your child's birthparents if you never discuss the details. Saying you will share pictures "often" may mean once a year to you, and once a day to the birthparents. Discuss how often you feel comfortable sharing photos, whether or not you want to have face-to-face visits, how often those visits might be, and so on. Nothing is more detrimental to the open adoption relationship than the adoptive parents and birthparents being on different pages. Specifics. Specifics. Specifics.

35. Do pass the baton when your child is mature enough.

While your child is a baby, the adults make all the adoption decisions. As the child matures, some of those responsibilities need to shift so the child is involved in making the decisions.

Be sensitive to your child's needs. Discuss with your spouse how you will feel if your child wants to see the birthparents more often than you like, or if the child wants to have less contact with them. There is no set age as to when the baton should be passed.

36. Do visit social media support groups.

Facebook and other social media sites are fantastic places to connect with others like you. There are public forums that will allow you to interact with all kinds of people.

There are also private sites where you will need an invitation to join a group of likeminded people. On those sites, you will be able to share and build each other up. Again, keep in mind that you should never say something on these pages that you do not want ever getting back to your child's birthparents.

Encourage your child's birthparents to join one of the many private birthparent pages.

There are all kinds of pages, though. Keep in mind that some have a tendency to shift toward the mean and nasty sides of adoption where birthparents attack adoptive parents, or adoptive parents say horrible things about birthparents. Stay away from those whose goal is to demonize others.

37. Don't put other adoption relationships in front of what you have with the birthparents.

It is natural for things to ebb and flow in the relationship you have with your child's birthparent. One day your relationship is perfect, and the next day they frustrate you. If you become close friends with your birthmother's sister, you are playing with fire. If you are going through a rough patch with one of the birthparents, you do not want someone caught in the middle of it. If your adoption comes to a point when you need to take a month off from contact but you are still hanging out with the birthmother's sister, you are asking for big trouble. Keep your relationship with the birthparents first, and let all the peripheral relationships take a backseat.

38. *Do decide how long your visits will be beforehand.*

This concept is more important in the early stages of the adoption relationship than later on. My experience is that things will run more smoothly if you plan beforehand how long a visit will last. We have had times when the birthparents could not get themselves to leave the child's presence and would stay hours after we wanted to go to bed. And we could not get ourselves to kick them out when they were so emotionally tied to the evening.

In our home, we let the birthparents have a big say in how long and how often the visits would be. When those decisions were made long enough beforehand, the birthparents were able to think clearly and not base their decisions on their emotions at the moment.

39. *Do open your adoption door slowly.*

It is common for adoptive parents to want to promise the world to the biological parents. The biological parents are giving you the greatest gift you will ever receive—parenthood—and you may feel like you need to do everything in your power to repay the favor.

Some adoptive parents promise too much, and once placement has occurred and the adoption relationship changes shape, they find themselves in an uncomfortable situation they had not anticipated.

Start your open adoption relationship off on the right foot. Promise only those things you know you can deliver. If you are not sure whether or not something is going to overwhelm you, do not promise it. You can always change your mind later and open up new parts of your adoption. Your relationship will never become damaged from providing *more* than you originally promised, but you might hurt your relationship if you close something that was previously open.

40. Don't expect your open adoption to eliminate a future identity crisis.

All kids, especially once they hit their teenage years, will go through a stage when they will need to figure out who they are. That is natural for everyone and it can be especially difficult for a child who was adopted.

Every child is different, so every child will process their history differently. Some children will see how much they are loved at home and they will not become overwhelmed with an identity crisis. Others will suffer greatly through an identity crisis no matter what you do as an adoptive parent.

Your job is to do the best you can. Talk about their adoption history in a way that they will understand how much they are loved. If you spend a lot of time talking negatively about their biological roots, there will be a good chance you child will internalize those negativities, thinking those things reflect who they are. If you do your best to show love toward your child's roots, you will have a better chance at building up those positives inside your child. You may not be able to escape a future identity crisis, but you can do your best to provide your child some tools if it does come.

41. *Don't try to do this alone.*

There is a good chance you will feel alone at times during your adoption process. Few, if any, of your closest family and friends have ever gone through something like this. That is okay. Take what you can get from those who love you. They may not fully understand, but they do know how to love you, and that is exactly what they want to do. Do not shut them out. If they say dumb things that show their ignorance of your situation, that is okay. They are doing their best.

42. *Do keep a blog while you are waiting to be chosen to adopt.*

You have already created an awesome profile that has been listed online and/or with your adoption agency. Even if your profile is fantastic, it is already weeks, months, or even years old. You need something current. You need somewhere a potential birthparent can go to see more about you—somewhere you are truly free to write as much as you want to—where your pictures and word count is not limited by the space the adoption agency has given you.

On top of bolstering your adoption profile, keeping a blog will also show any potential birthparent that you are willing to share yourself. If someone is considering you to adopt their child, and they want to know if you are able to put forth the effort to take and share photos, your blog is immediate proof of that even before they contact you.

43. Do talk openly and freely with your child about adoption.

Do not avoid talking about adoption. Do not treat the subject like it is taboo. You want your children to embrace their adoption history, so why would you ever avoid it in conversation? Talk about it often. Talk about it fondly. Do this from the time they are young, even before they are able to understand what you are saying. Do not ever let yourself get stuck in a situation where you do not know how to break the news to them. Create an atmosphere of openness in your home where your children know they can talk freely about their history. You cannot expect them to embrace their history if they do not feel free to talk about it.

44. *Do become familiar with your local adoption laws.*

In the United States, adoption laws are decided on the state level, so every state will have different requirements and restrictions. Some of the differences are not a big deal, such as how many education hours you must complete before being allowed to adopt, but others are very important. For example, in my home state of Idaho, it is common to bring a gift to the expecting mother while she is at the hospital. In other states that type of behavior is strictly forbidden since some see it as a form of coercion to pressure the expecting parents toward adoption, and giving a gift would land you in serious trouble.

If your adoption takes place in a different state than where you live, you will especially need to pay attention to the laws. Talk to your agency caseworker and get in contact with a good attorney who knows the ins-and-outs of adoption.

45. *Do decide in advance how much you want your own extended family involved.*

God picked your family for you. You did not have a say in the matter, but you do get to choose how much your family is involved with your adoption relationship.

There is nothing wrong with keeping things simple. Your sister does not have to be good friends with your child's birthmother. You do not have to invite the birthfather to your family reunion just because you consider him part of your family. Always keep in mind that the greater number of people involved in your adoption, the more complicated you situation will become. And the more complicated your situation becomes, the harder it is to control. You will have no control over what Crazy Uncle Joe says to the birthmother when he has her cornered.

Many extended families are already riddled with drama, and many adoptions are already also riddled with drama. If you choose to bring these two elements together, you better be sure you know what you are doing. If some drama occurs between your child's birthmother and your sister—if someone's feelings get hurt—whose side are you going to take? That would be a lose-lose situation. It is not always a bad thing to let your extended family mingle with your child's birthparents, but you know your family and you know their propensity for drama. Go with your instinct, and do not let your family pressure you to change your mind. This decision is yours to make, not theirs.

46. *Do be careful in making a decision about connecting on social media.*

You already share so much of your life with your child's biological family. If you choose to connect on social media sites like Facebook and Instagram, you are choosing to open your adoption door almost all the way. Some people feel this is the best way to keep contact casual and free. Others feel it completely takes away their ability to have a private life.

Adoptive parents tend to obsess over their child's birthparents social media pages. If you are social media friends, you will have access to everything they post. Resist the urge to perpetually check their status. If your child's birthfather is having a hard day, you may feel you are somehow responsible, even if his troubles are not related to adoption. If your child's birthmother is making poor decisions, you may feel affected by it. Give them some space. Let them live their lives. Do not follow their every move or obsess over them.

And if you think they are not equally interested in your life, you are probably wrong. They are just as interested in you as you are in them—maybe even more so because they want to follow the life of their biological child. Your privacy is limited.

Again, it is common for people to connect on social media sites, and it works out well for many of them, but you must decide what works for you. Are you the type of personality who can give them their space, or will you obsess over them? You should consider these things long before becoming Facebook friends, because you can damage your relationship by "unfriending" someone who has become used to following your page.

47. Don't let your struggles shake your faith in God.

God did not curse you with infertility because you are unworthy of being a parent. God loves you just as much as He does the lady next door with nine kids. Do not look at your infertility as a curse. Look at it as God's way of telling you He is calling you to something different. Adoptive parents have a special and unique role in this world, and we are every bit as important in God's plan as those who have children born to them naturally.

48. Don't write off others' opinions just because they have never been in your shoes.

Your situation is unique. That's true. Few people have been in your shoes. That's true too. But that does not mean others cannot be right about something. Listen to what others have to say. If they are wrong, do not take their advice. If they are right, their words may just help you.

49. Do say "thank you" when the other side sacrifices.

Some gifts are easy to notice, like when someone gives you a nice present on your birthday. Other gifts are a lot more subtle. If your child's birthparent ever compliments you on something you have done as a parent, that is their way of showing their appreciation for what you do. Make a big deal about it. Tell them, "Thank you so much. That means the world coming from you." If they send a gift on your child's first birthday, that is their way of saying they believe they made the right decision in placing that child in your home. Make a big deal out of it. If your child's birthparent ever refers to you as "The Mom" or "The Dad," that is their way of sustaining who you are. Thank them. Nobody likes to feel like their words or deeds go unnoticed or unappreciated. These simple words are essential for any symbiotic relationship.

50. Don't talk about your infertility woes like you deserve someone's pity in your adoption profile.

Many potential birthparents want to know about your infertility because they want to know your reasons for choosing adoption, but that does not mean you should go looking for pity. Expecting parents who find themselves considering whether or not to place their child for adoption have a lot on their plate already. They do not need to hear all about your woes. Write a sentence or two about your infertility in your adoption profile, answer any questions the expecting parents have, and then move on. As difficult as your infertility is, it is not as tough as what the expecting parents are going through.

51. *Do fill out your adoption paperwork as quickly as you can.*

There is a chance you will have to wait a long time before being chosen to adopt. There is also a chance you could be chosen quickly. You may miss an opportunity to be chosen if you drag your feet.

Adoption paperwork takes a long time. When my wife and I were in the process of adoption for a second time, we I spent every free minute working on our paperwork because we did not want to miss any opportunity God might send our way. It is common for hopeful adoptive couples to take months and months to finish their paperwork, but we finished everything in just over a month. If we had taken even two weeks longer, we would have missed the opportunity to adopt our little girl, Hazel. We were discovered by Hazel's biological mother a few weeks after our profile went online, contacted a week after that, and baby Hazel was in our arms three weeks after that. It was a total of seven weeks between the time our homestudy was completed and when we brought baby Hazel home with us. If we had taken a long time with our paperwork, who knows how long our wait might have been?

52. *Do discuss pictures and updates often.*

Even if you had this discussion long before the adoption took place, understand that people's needs change over time. Adoptive parents tend to become more lax with the frequency of sharing as the years go by. For some situations, that is okay. The birthparents may not need as many photos as they did in the days soon after placement. In other adoption relationships this can be detrimental. Make sure you are communicating. Do not ever let laziness be your reason for not sharing pictures. If for whatever reason you have not been as diligent in sharing as you used to, make sure the birthparents know it is not because you do not care about them. Talk to them about whether or not their needs are being met. Talk to them about whether or not you feel overwhelmed with how often you are sharing. This can be a complicated part of your relationship, but it does not have to be if both sides are willing to consider the other's feelings.

53. Don't just assume your child has come to terms with adoption.

Talk about adoption often. Find out what your child is thinking. Is your situation too intense for your child's wellbeing? Would your child like to see the birthparents more often? Less often? Find these things out. Help your children cope and discover who they are. Help them embrace their history. Help them understand that their life is built on love, not abandonment.

54. Don't sidestep the birthparents if you are in contact with others.

The relationship you have with your child's birthparents should always be in front of your relationship with their family and friends. If you create a blog to share pictures and updates, give the blog password only to the birthparents and leave it up to them to decide who has access to it. If one of their friends contacts you for the password, you tell them it is not yours to give away.

If the birthfather's parents want to come visit, make sure he knows about it. If the birthmother's friends want to connect with you on social media, make sure the birthmother knows.

Their situation is complicated, and you do not want to be the cause for more drama.

55. *Don't forget your needs matter too.*

Someone gave you the most amazing gift you will ever receive—parenthood. You cannot possibly repay that, but you should do your best to create a healthy open adoption. Part of keeping your adoption healthy means serving others, but it also means you need to take care of yourself. Your needs still matter. Your sanity matters. If you ever find yourself at your wits end, you must communicate that with the birthparents. If you spend too much energy worrying about everybody but yourself, you will get to a point where you cannot take it anymore and everything will fall apart. Find a balance. Communicate your needs.

56. *Don't discourage your child from coping.*

Your child will need to come to terms with adoption in the way he or she feels best. That might mean something completely different than what you have envisioned. If your child wants to talk about it, do it. If your child does not want to talk about it, wait until they are ready. The same goes for face-to-face visits, exchanging letters, etc. The older your child gets, the more you will need to let loose of their reins and let them do things their way.

57. Become familiar with adoption terminology.

Even after years of being an advocate for adoption, I am sure I have offended someone with the way I have worded something in this book. The first edition of my book *Open Adoption, Open Heart* is quite different from the second edition because I learned how to properly use terms like "birthmother" and "expecting mother."

Adoption is such a fragile subject that we always run the risk of wording something poorly when we talk about it. Do not be offended when others make mistakes. Educate them, but be tactful with you words. In order to do so, you must educate yourself first. You can find lengthy lists of proper terminology on sites like adoption.com.

58. Do council with someone through the process to ensure you do not do something stupid.

If you are doing a private adoption, get in contact with a lawyer from the start. If you are going through an agency, establish a good line of communication with a caseworker. You do not need to call them every day. Just make sure you have a line open with them when you make big decisions. You are probably a rookie at this game. They are not.

59. Do set boundaries if the birthparents live nearby.

Adoption relationships inherently have a high level of intensity. That is not necessarily a bad thing. Oftentimes those intense emotions are high levels of love, but any relationship with such intensity also carries with it a propensity for exhaustion. If your child's birthparents live close to your home and you have established a situation where they are free to drop in at any time for a visit, you are leaving yourself wide open for fatigue.

Our daughter's birthmother lived across town and worked only about two miles from our home. Sometimes she would stop by on her lunch break or after work. We found ourselves wondering every day if she would show up, and that was too much for us. Our relationship was built on love, but sometimes too much of a good thing burned us out. We set some boundaries. We still saw her just as often, but since we had guidelines set about when she would and would not come, we were able to relax more. It made our everyday life a whole lot easier.

60. Do find joy in knowing you are providing the very thing the birthparents want.

You were chosen to raise this child for a reason. Your child's birthparents want the best for this child, and you should find joy in being able to provide that. It is common for adoptive parents to feel guilty about their joy when they see the birthparents hurting.

Find joy in your role. Find joy in being a loving parent. Find joy in being the very thing the birthparents want most for their child.

61. Do understand that the biological grandparents may not see you as the parents.

The birthmother's family watched her belly grow larger and larger. They supported her through the physical and emotional trials of pregnancy. It is natural for the biological family to think of this child as the offspring of their own family tree before they consider the child as "yours." That is natural. This is especially true in the early years. That does not mean they do not sustain you in your role as this child's parents, but understanding this may help shed some light on why they do or say certain things. Hopefully this does not get in the way of your relationship, but if it makes your situation overly uncomfortable, you may need to address it. If that happens, be especially careful to be tactful, understanding, and never do it without the birthparents being involved. They have had a relationship with their family much longer than you have and they know how to talk to them.

62. *Do expect the relationship with the biological parents to change after placement.*

If you are lucky enough to have contact with the biological parents before the birth, you will have opportunity to develop a loving relationship early on. In those early days, the biological parents hold all of the "power" in the relationship. If they change their mind about adoption, there will be nothing you can do about it, and that is their right. Once the adoption is final, that power shifts to your hands. If you make a decision about the openness in their adoption, there is not a whole lot they can do about it. This transition of power will change the nature of your relationship. That does not mean your relationship will inevitably fall apart, but things do change. If you are expecting that to happen, the transition can be smooth.

In some cases the expecting parents have had a relationship with the hopeful adoptive parents for a long time. Such is the case when a child is placed into the arms of a relative or family friend. Understand that the nature of that relationship will change after the adoption takes place. Again, that does not mean the relationship will fall apart, but things will definitely be different than they were before.

63. *Don't forget about Birthdad.*

A birthfather can be a valuable part of a child's life, but birthfathers are often left out of the picture. Men handle things differently than women do, and some cope by creating space between them and the adoption. Do not automatically take this as reason to exclude the birthfather from your adoption triad.

It is common for the biological mother and father to separate before the adoption takes place. If that is the case, chances are you will have more contact with the biological mother since she is the one carrying the child. It is also possible that their reason for separating has left a bitter taste in her mouth regarding the biological father. Do not let her negative view of him determine your relationship with him. Your relationship with the birthfather should not affect your relationship with the birthmother. They do not have to be in the same room together. He may be a wonderful man who could be a positive influence in your child's life.

64. *Don't tell other people how open their adoption should be.*

Your situation is unique. You already know that. This also means other people's situations are unique. You do not want anyone telling you how to manage your open adoption relationship, so do not push your views on others. This does not mean you do not talk to others about their adoption. It just means that at the end of the day their decisions are their own to make, and you should never judge them for what they feel is right for their family.

65. *Don't expect open adoption to be easy.*

Plan on it being hard. It is. Even those who make it look easy go through difficult times. The more open the relationship is, the more vulnerable everyone is to difficult times and hurt feelings. Do not ever let your insecurities and discomfort be reason to close the adoption. Things that are worthwhile are often difficult.

66. Don't live through the biological parents' pregnancy because you cannot get pregnant.

If you watch your child's biological mother's pregnancy through the eyes of jealousy, that jealousy might become a wall between you. This can be easier said than done. Talk to others who have been in your shoes. Find joy in your own journey. Find joy in the fact that you feel called to be an adoptive parent. Focus on the blessings you have, and not on the experiences you will never go through.

67. Do keep the first visits simple.

When that baby comes into the world, there will be a lot of people anxious to meet him or her. If you plan to have face-to-face visits, do your best to keep these first visits simple. It may be hard for some people to understand why they are not invited, but your situation is already complicated enough.

Try to picture how you will feel if a lot of people want to pass the baby around and you hardly get a turn. If you are okay with that, then by all means, plan your visit accordingly. If you are unsure how that will make you feel, plan things on the safe side.

You must also keep in mind that the birthparents might get overwhelmed with a large gathering. Birthparents experience a whirlwind of emotions, especially during those first few visits, and having a bunch of people present will make things even more intense.

Whether the first visit takes place a day after placement or when your child turns eighteen, that first visit can be very intense. Plan accordingly.

68. Do talk to your child about how much you love their birthparents.

Nothing will help your child embrace their adoption history like showing them that you love their biological parents. If you do this, they will be more likely to embrace that relationship as well, and they will have an easier time with their identity because of it.

69. Do remember that you are trusted to make the decisions.

You were chosen to be the parents of this child. It is nice to have the approval of the birthparents when you make decisions, but you have to make decisions according to your own conscience. Open adoption is not co-parenting. There is no need to ask the birthparents' permission before making major decisions. The decisions are yours to make.

70. Do excuse yourself from the delivery room if the biological parents need time.

If you are lucky enough to be invited to the hospital, do not be overbearing. You are a guest. That child is not yours, even if you are confident the adoption will take place. If the biological parents want time alone with the child, you must give them the opportunity to do so. This can be difficult for some hopeful adoptive parents since more time together with the baby can mean more time bonding. And more time bonding makes hopeful adoptive couples scared that the biological parents will not choose adoption. It is natural to feel scared of this bonding time, and your fears are not unfounded. There is a chance the biological parents may change their mind, but they have the right to do so. You must give them their space and time with the child if they want it. If this adoption is meant to be, the time they spend with their child can be a powerful time together. Time spent alone with the child can help give them the tools they need to come to terms with their difficult time.

71. *Don't get too enveloped in your own difficult times.*

It is hard to recognize the fact that other people are going through something difficult if we focus only on ourselves. The time surrounding placement is a time when everyone's emotions are at their peak. It is important to keep others' emotions in mind during the difficult times. You may not be the only person struggling with something, and if you do not acknowledge that fact, your relationships can be damaged. Worry about yourself, but consider other people too.

72. *Don't expect the hospital staff to understand your adoption situation.*

If you are lucky enough to be invited to the hospital, keep in mind that the hospital staff may not be educated on adoption.

When my wife and I adopted our son, the staff was fantastic. The hospital where he was delivered had been chosen because the adoption agency recommended it from previous adoption experiences. But our experience with the hospital staff from our daughter's adoption was quite different. The nurses and desk staff were not accommodating or understanding about our unusual circumstances. They said awkward and insensitive things to us as well as to the biological parents. They asked the wrong people permission for different things like vaccinations and treatments. They became agitated with us when we corrected them. Do your best to keep the situation as comfortable as possible, focusing on the needs of the biological parents first and foremost.

73. *Do find humor in your situation.*

You will have plenty of uncomfortable situations come your way. And as the old saying goes: Crisis plus time equals humor. But why not laugh about things now? When someone says something horribly insensitive, laugh about it when you get back to the car. When someone sees your one-month-old baby and compliments you on how quickly you lost your baby weight, smile and say, "The trick is to eat a lot of pickled ochre." Find joy in your journey wherever you can. It makes the hard times easier.

74. Do take an interest in the birthparents life outside of adoption.

You love your child's birthparents, and not just because they gave you the gift of parenthood. Take an interest in their life outside of adoption. If they love horses, talk about horses, even if you cannot tell the difference between a horse and a goat. Talk about their new job. Talk about their new college roommate. I have seen more than one adoption triad struggle to connect but later blossom after discovering this.

75. Do expect your teenager to say something hurtful someday.

Hopefully this never happens to you, but there is a good chance it will. Teenagers are still kids. I remember throwing temper tantrums when I was a teen—they just did not take on the same form as those I threw when I was a toddler. Teenager tantrums are aimed right at their parents' hearts, jabbing where they know they will get a reaction. Even some of the best adoptive parents have heard their angry child say, "I would have been happier growing up with my birthmom." Do not take it personally. They still love you. You are still an awesome parent. They are just trying to get under your skin.

76. Don't start any level of openness that will exhaust you unless you know it will not last.

Giving too much of yourself will exhaust you. You will get to a point where you just will not want to—or just cannot—do it anymore. You should avoid taking on an exhausting amount of openness... with one exception. It is okay to promise something huge if you do it in short spurts. It is okay to promise a ton of pictures during that first month if both sides know it will not continue like that. It is okay to allow a long visit if you know it does not happen very often. You know your limits. You know what you can handle. Just remember to communicate about it.

77. Do spend a lot of time on your adoption profile (aka "Dear Birthmother Letter")

I know. I know. Some people hate the term "Dear Birthmother letter" because the person you are addressing hasn't given birth and thus is not technically a birthmother yet. But that is the term most used by many adoption agencies. It is also known as the Adoption Profile letter, Dear Potential Birthmother letter, Dear Expecting Parents letter, etc.

Spend a lot of time on this letter to get it right. This may be your only chance to make that first impression on someone considering you to raise their child, and if you do not shine you will be passed up. Use quality photos. If you are a terrible writer, find a friend to help you write it and proofread proofread proofread.

78. Do read and learn as much as you can about adoption.

There are all kinds of books you can read. Read people's stories. Read books with advice. Read people's blogs. Read the discussions that take place in forums on the internet. Once you are chosen to adopt you will find out just how little you know. Do not be so thick as to think you can learn everything as you go. If you get off on the wrong foot with your relationship, you may have a hard time correcting it. The life and wellbeing of your child depends on how much effort you put into this. Do not be lazy. Do not be too busy. You owe it to yourself, the biological parents, and especially to your child.

If you would like to read book one of my Glass Half-Full Adoption Memoirs series, *Open Adoption, Open Heart*, which is the story of our first adoption, all you have to do is email me and I will email you a digital version for free so you can read it on your digital reader.

79. *Don't be afraid to share pictures of yourself loving this child.*

Many adoptive parents are uncomfortable sharing pictures where the child is being smothered with love. Some think it is too "in-their-face" to share those things.

First of all, it is not too in-their-face. They chose you to love and raise this child, and that is exactly what you are doing. So, why would not share pictures of you doing exactly what they want you to do?

Secondly, it may hurt them to see their child in someone else's arms, but that is a good thing. Facing this pain by seeing you together can be a good tool to help them progress. Obviously, do not go overboard or you will indeed be too "in-their-face" with what you have and what they do not.

80. *Don't take it personally if your child wants to cuddle with the birthparents during a visit.*

Some kids are cuddly. Some are not. Some kids prefer to cuddle only with Mom and Dad, others love to be held by strangers. Do not worry if your kid wants to spend the majority of your visit on the lap of the birthparents. This does not mean your child does not love you. This does not mean they care more about their birthparents than they do about you. This does not mean you are unimportant. It just means they are enjoying the attention. Do not read into it any further than that.

81. Do understand that the hospital time belongs to the biological parents.

The biological parents should be in charge of who is invited to the hospital. You do not invite yourself. If you are lucky enough to be invited, you do not invite your friends or family. If they do give you permission to invite some people, do not go overboard. Do not throw a big party. Do not flood the room with people. Keep everything reverent and simple. The time at the hospital is usually the most delicate part of the whole process. That is where the biological parents must face the reality of their decision. Remember that you are a guest there.

82. *Don't just share pictures with your hair done perfectly.*

Be real when you are sharing pictures. You know the birth-parents took a big leap of faith when they chose you to raise their child, and deep down inside you want to prove they made the right choice, but do not let that stop you from being who you really are. They want to see you cuddling with your kids while you wear your Spongebob flannel PJ's. They want to see you caked in mud after getting caught in the rain at the park. They placed their child with a real family, not with the Brady Bunch. You are not perfect, and they do not want you to pretend you are.

83. *Don't give the expecting parents a bunch of money.*

We would all like to believe that everyone around us is honest. We would all like to have faith in our fellow man—believing that nobody would stoop so low as to con hopeful adoptive parents out of money. Do not be so foolish. Hopeful adoptive parents are easy targets because they want parenthood so badly they would do almost anything to get it. My wife and I have gone through the adoption process twice, and during those two times we had people try to trick us on three different occasions. Two of those times were young women claiming to be pregnant when they were not, and the other time was someone online posing as an expecting mother.

If you suspect someone is being dishonest with you, contact your adoption lawyer or caseworker. Any caseworker worth a grain of salt can spot the tell-tale signs of a scammer.

In some states it is okay to give money to an expecting parent in order to help with hospital bills and pregnancy expenses. Be sure you know your state's laws regarding these matters because it is strictly forbidden in some states and can land you in a lot of hot water. If you live in a state where it is permitted, you are more likely to be a target. Cover your bases. Talk often with your caseworker if any money at all is given for support.

Also keep in mind that if the adoption falls through you will likely never see that money again. Very few agencies will refund your money, and it is even less likely you will ever get it back from those you gave it to.

84. Do be willing to say, "Now, that's just not helpful."

This is a phrase I learned from one of my friends who hosts an adoption radio program, and it comes in handy. There are plenty of people in this world who talk before thinking. There are also countless people who know what they are saying will be hurtful, but they say it anyway. And there are tons of people who do not mean to hurt your feelings, but they do not know what they are talking about. When someone says something outrageous about infertility or adoption, and you do not know how to respond, just say, "Now, that's just not helpful."

85. Don't forget that you and the birthparents are not the only ones in this adoption triad.

It is called a triad for a reason. There are three parts to it: the adoptive parents, birthparents, and *the child*. During the first few years, a baby or toddler does not have an opinion about adoption. All of the adoption discussion takes place between the adults. Children begin to think for themselves as they grow older. If you are the type of person who talks about adoption everywhere you go, and your son asks you to stop telling everyone he is adopted, then for goodness' sake, stop telling everyone. If your daughter thinks you have too many or too few visits with her birthfather, you need to take her needs into account.

86. Don't adopt if you do not want to.

The only people who should adopt are those who want to. If you feel compelled because you cannot become a parent any other way, do not adopt. If you feel that adoption is inferior to raising a child you gave birth to, do not adopt. One of my friends always says, "Adoption was not our plan B. It was the plan that was meant to be." If you do not feel this way, do not adopt.

87. Do understand that the first year is the hardest.

Things will get easier over time. Many adoptive parents ask themselves during that time how long they can keep this up. They are exhausted by the perpetual height of emotions. They are worn out because their relationship is not going how they had envisioned. Wounds take time to heal. Relationships take time to develop. Life takes time to become normal again. Adoption is not easy, especially during that first year. This does not mean that the second year is easy, but it will be much easier than that first. And the third year is easier than the second.

88. Don't close part of the adoption without communicating about it.

Nothing hurts more than taking away part of a relationship when someone has grown to depend on it. Whether it is social media, or face-to-face visits, do not make major changes to your relationship without discussing it with the birthparents. Respect them enough to communicate.

89. Do embrace what you are.

Embrace your role and do not focus on what you are not. You are an adoptive parent. You will not be called to anything greater in this life. Focus on that. It is okay that your child does not share your genes. You provide a contribution to the human race that few people get to do. The world needs people like you. You are not inferior to other people because your body lacks the ability to make a baby. You are not inferior as a parent because this child did not grow inside of you. The sooner you can embrace what you are, the sooner you can let go of the things you are not.

90. Don't ever feel guilty for "letting others down" with your infertility.

My wife and I felt bad that we jumped ship on our infertility treatments when we still had options left. The nurse we had been working with really wanted to help us get pregnant. That does not matter. Our decision to stop treatments was the right one for us, and that was what mattered. It does not matter what others feel you should do. They are not in our shoes.

91. Don't make important decisions while your emotions are elevated.

I cannot stress this point enough. When something goes wrong in your adoption relationship, do not just react without taking a step back and thinking things through. When someone contacts you and your mind floods with wonderful possibilities, do not start making promises you cannot keep. Your adoption journey is going to take you through some of the highest highs and the lowest lows you will ever feel in life. When you feel your emotions elevated, whether positively or negatively, take a step back. Take time to make your decisions, even if that means you will need weeks or months to do so. It is hard to reverse big decisions once you have already put them into action.

92. *Don't take over other people's roles at the hospital.*

If you are lucky enough to be invited to the hospital, remember that you are a guest. Feel free to ask if there is any way you can be of service, but do not jump into a role that is not yours. If the biological mother's parents or best friend are present, they will probably be the main support. Let them. You are a guest. Do not be in the way.

93. *Don't make promises you are not sure you can keep.*

You may want to promise the world because you feel you owe the birthparents your life. You do not. You cannot possibly pay them back, so do not kill yourself trying. Do the best you can do. Spend a lot of time learning, pondering, praying, meditating—whatever you do when you make major life decisions. Take these things seriously, so when it is time to make promises you will not jump into a commitment you cannot keep. And do not ever make a promise you do not intend to keep simply because you want something. That should go without saying, but that is exactly what some selfish people do.

94. *Don't wear yourself out thinking too much about adoption.*

When your life gets too flooded with adoption related things, find something else to do. My wife and I used to take walks together where we would set aside an hour in which we were not allowed to talk about adoption. We had to do this because we were so engulfed in the process that we struggled to think about anything else. Even during the good times it can be overwhelming.

95. *Don't smother or pressure an expecting mother.*

You should never approach an expecting mother (or father) in hopes of convincing her to place her baby for adoption. If you meet a pregnant woman, it is not your place to tell her someone else should raise her child. If she has questions for you, by all means you should talk to her about it, but unless she is your sister, daughter, or close friend, it is not your place to bring these things up. She has enough on her plate as she tries to figure out what she wants to do with her life. She does not need you pressuring her into something, no matter how badly you want to become a parent.

96. *Don't force the birthparents to be in contact with each other.*

If the relationship between the birthfather and birthmother has gone sour, do not force them into contact with each other. Do not invite them both to the same event without telling them they should expect to see the other. Consider changing the way you share pictures and updates if you have a blog where they both leave comments. Forcing them together may make their life needlessly uncomfortable, and you do not want to be caught in the middle of it. Most of all, your child should not be caught in the middle of it.

97. *Don't be afraid to say, "I don't know."*

You know that you should learn as much as you can about adoption. You are reading every blog and every book you can find on the subject. Still, you do not know everything. It is okay to say you do not know if someone asks you what you want. It is okay to say you do not know if a decision makes you uncomfortable. It is *not* okay to make big decisions and offer someone something you will soon be taking away.

71

98. *Do talk to everyone about adoption.*

People in the world do not think about adoption as often as they should. When a woman becomes unexpectedly pregnant, she should not think the only two options are to raise the child or have an abortion. And if they do think of adoption, they must understand that there are all kinds of adoptions—open, closed, somewhere in between. The world needs to you to open your mouth. Adoption is no longer a topic of taboo like it was in the 1960's. Talk about it. Talk about it. Talk about it.

99. *Don't give up.*

www.ingramcontent.com/pod-product-compliance
Lightning Source LLC
Chambersburg PA
CBHW071930020426
42331CB00010B/2794